TABLE OF CONTENTS

Venus hits back a shot at the final of the 2001 U.S. Open.

A GRAND SLAM MOMENT

Huge lights lit up **Center Court.** The most important tennis **matches** take place there. The event was the 2001 women's **final** of the **U.S. Open,** one of the four international **Grand Slam** events.

Venus & Serena Williams

By Madeline Donaldson

AMAZING
ATHLETES

LERNER**SPORTS** / **Minneapolis**

This book is available in two editions:
Library binding by LernerSports
Soft cover by First Avenue Editions
Imprints of Lerner Publishing Group
241 First Avenue North
Minneapolis, MN 55401 U.S.A.

Website address: www.lernerbooks.com

Library of Congress Cataloging-in-Publication Data

Donaldson, Madeline.
    Venus & Serena Williams / by Madeline Donaldson.
        p.   cm. — (Amazing athletes)
    Includes bibliographical references and index.
    ISBN: 0-8225-3316-2 (lib. bdg. : alk. paper)
    ISBN: 0-8225-9842-6 (pbk. : alk. paper)
    1. Williams, Venus, 1980—Juvenile literature. 2. Williams, Serena, 1981—Juvenile literature.
3. Tennis players—United States—Biography—Juvenile literature. [1. Williams, Venus, 1980-
2. Williams, Serena, 1981- 3. Tennis players. 4. African Americans—Biography. 5. Women—
Biography.] I. Title. II. Series.
    GV994.A1 D65 2003
    796.342'092'2—dc21
                                                                        2002003284

Manufactured in the United States of America
1 2 3 4 5 6 – DP – 08 07 06 05 04 03

For the first time, two African Americans were to face each other for the title. Both had played hard to get to the final. Both were sure they could win. Venus and Serena Williams also just happened to be sisters. And they were also best friends. Both found it stressful to play one another, because one sister would have to lose.

Serena shouts as she slams the ball over the net.

The sisters pose with Billie Jean King before the final. King was a tennis great in the 1960s and 1970s.

The crowd roared after the patriotic song "God Bless America" was sung by Diana Ross and a choir. Fireworks went off. Then Venus and Serena warmed up, hitting balls back and forth as they'd done so many times before.

Diana Ross was the lead singer of a famous 1960s girl group called The Supremes.

Venus, at six feet one inch tall, is known for her monster **serve.** Serena, at five feet ten inches, can belt her powerful shots just about anywhere on the court. But on this night, the stress may have been too much. Neither sister played as well as she could have. Venus beat Serena in straight **sets** to win her second U.S. Open title. Still, these two young African Americans, who'd grown up in a California **ghetto,** were proud of making it to their country's tennis final.

The last time sisters played one another in a Grand Slam final was in 1884!

Venus *(left)* and Serena *(right)* started playing tennis when they were very young. Their father, Richard, was their first coach.

Growing Up in the Ghetto

Venus and Serena Williams grew up in Compton, a town in southern California. They were the youngest of five daughters. Their dad, Richard, had caught the tennis bug. He had been teaching their older sisters to play tennis.

In 1984, when Venus was four, she started hitting tennis balls with her family. A year later, when Serena turned four, she also picked up a racket for the first time. Before long, it was clear the two girls had a lot of natural talent. Their early skills amazed Richard and his wife, Oracene.

Walls in the ghettos of Los Angeles often were covered with graffiti.

The Williamses' neighborhood was in a part of Compton that had high crime rates. Gang violence was common. The neighborhood's tennis courts weren't in great shape. The Williams sisters had to be careful when they practiced. Sometimes fights broke out between the gangs near the courts, and the girls would have to leave. But the danger didn't stop them from going to the courts nearly every day.

Richard wanted his daughters to be great tennis players. But he also wanted them to do well in school. He told Venus and Serena they couldn't play tennis if they hadn't done their homework. Both sisters worked hard at tennis and in school.

Over time, gang members came to respect what Richard and his daughters were doing on Compton's cracked courts. The gangs left them alone.

On Compton's courts, Richard pushes Venus in a ball-filled shopping cart.

Serena cracks a serve in a tournament in 1990. The media had a lot of interest in the sisters' tennis progress.

GETTING ATTENTION

Venus was the older sister by a little over a year. At age nine, she began playing in and winning junior tennis **tournaments.** By age ten, she had won the Southern California championship for girls twelve and younger. At the same time, Serena was also winning tournaments. Both girls were drawing a lot of attention from the media—magazines, newspapers, and television.

Media attention made it hard for Venus and Serena to focus on schoolwork. They changed schools three times to escape the attention. But the media continued to follow them around.

Richard decided Venus and Serena should stop playing in junior tournaments. Venus left the junior **tennis tour,** or circuit, undefeated at age eleven. Serena, age ten, had been beaten only three times.

Venus and Serena's older sisters are Yetunde, Isha, and Lyndrea.

Venus's tennis skills wowed a lot of professional coaches.

TURNING PROFESSIONAL

Venus and Serena kept practicing, although they didn't play in tournaments. With their dad coaching them, they got better and better. They improved in both **singles** (when one person plays another) and **doubles** (when two

two-person teams play). But after many months of coaching, Richard felt he'd done what he could. His daughters needed a better coach.

Many coaches had heard about the Williams sisters. Richard and Oracene sometimes let coaches watch the girls practice. Rick Macci, a professional coach from Florida, flew to California. He couldn't believe how good Venus was. He called her "a female Michael Jordan."

Rick Macci (*left*) coached Venus (*right*) and Serena from 1991 to 1995. About Venus, he once said, "There wasn't a day she wouldn't hit 200 serves."

Rick lived in Florida, where coaching cost a lot of money. Venus and Serena's parents talked about what to do. Should they move so the girls could be coached? Richard and Oracene decided to quit their jobs and move the entire family to Florida. Coach Macci had agreed to train the girls for free.

They practiced many hours each day. They got stronger and gained more experience in singles and doubles. Instead of going to school, the girls were taught at home.

Venus and Serena's parents were still serious about education. They wanted their daughters to be smart people, not just smart tennis players. The girls still couldn't compete in tournaments.

In 1994, when Venus was about fourteen, she started bugging her parents about turning

professional. Venus wanted her chance to play against the best women players. As she told a magazine, "I'm strong, I'm tall, I work hard on the court." Her parents finally gave their OK. But she could only play in a certain number of tournaments a year. The same limits were put on Serena when she turned pro the next year.

In October 1994, Venus played her first match as a professional. She won!

Companies approached the Williamses with offers of money if Venus would **endorse** (help sell) their products. The family signed a contract with Reebok, a company that makes sports equipment. The endorsement money helped pay for travel, housing, training partners, and other expenses.

Venus holds up tennis shoes made by Reebok. She first agreed to endorse Reebok products in 1995.

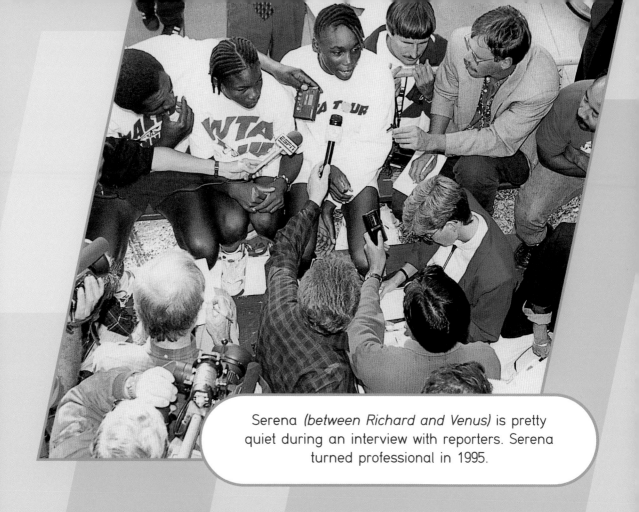

Serena *(between Richard and Venus)* is pretty quiet during an interview with reporters. Serena turned professional in 1995.

RISING THROUGH THE RANKS

Venus and Serena played fewer matches than other professionals on the women's tennis circuit. Each girl had some wins and some losses. They continued to practice and train.

After a few years, both girls were ranked in the top 100 by the **Women's Tennis Association (WTA).** This group ranks players based on their performance at tournaments.

Venus and Serena were playing some of the best players on the tour, such as Martina Hingis and Lindsay Davenport.

Venus and Serena graduated from the Driftwood Academy in Florida. Both earned good grades.

School was still a huge priority. Venus graduated from high school in 1997. This big step was paired with success on the court. She made it to her first Grand Slam final, the 1997 U.S. Open. She lost to Martina Hingis.

Serena graduated from high school in 1998. That year, they both headed for Australia for another Grand Slam event, the Australian

Open. They won their opening matches. Then they had to play each other for the first time as professionals. Neither liked the experience much. "It wasn't so funny, eliminating my little sister," Venus said after beating Serena.

In 1998, the sisters played one another in a professional match for the first time. Each played hard, but Venus won.

No matter what happens on the court, Venus and Serena remain best friends. They enjoy each other's tennis success.

TENNIS SISTERS, TENNIS RIVALS

Venus and Serena enjoyed lots of success in the late 1990s and early 2000s. Their dad encouraged them to play in separate tournaments whenever they could. This cut down on the stress and the bad feelings when one of them had to lose to the other.

The Williams sisters also made time for fun. They both liked music and video games. They rarely turned down a chance to go shopping. And they stayed in touch by e-mail when they weren't playing in the same tournaments.

Serena struggled through her 1999 final match at the U.S. Open. She finally beat Martina Hingis to win the sisters' first singles Grand Slam.

Serena beat her sister for the first time in a 1999 final in Munich, Germany.

Sometimes a tournament was too important for either of them to miss. For a while, Venus had the edge and won most of the head-to-head matches. Serena kept calm, saying, "Family comes first, no matter how many times we play each other."

Serena got to the finals of the 1999 U.S. Open. She beat Martina Hingis and became the first Williams sister to win a Grand Slam singles event.

In 2000 Venus won her first singles title at Wimbledon, a Grand Slam event held in England. She also added her own singles win at the U.S. Open. The sisters represented the United States at the Summer Olympic Games in Australia. They each took home a gold medal for their doubles play. Venus also won a gold in singles. Of the doubles win, Venus said, "This is almost bigger than singles . . . because I have this victory with Serena, my sister, . . . my best friend."

Venus and Serena proudly show off their gold medals from the 2000 Olympics.

The 2001 U.S. Open was the first time the Williams sisters played against one another in a Grand Slam final. The media attention was crazy. The match was televised at night in **prime time** (the most-watched hours). Richard stayed away, but Oracene was in the stands. In the end, Venus again beat Serena.

Oracene was on hand again in Paris, London, and New York in 2002. Her daughters played in the finals of the French Open, Wimbledon, and the U.S. Open. Serena won all three events. She ended the year ranked number one in the world! Venus nailed the number two spot.

Serena holds up the 2002 French Open trophy.

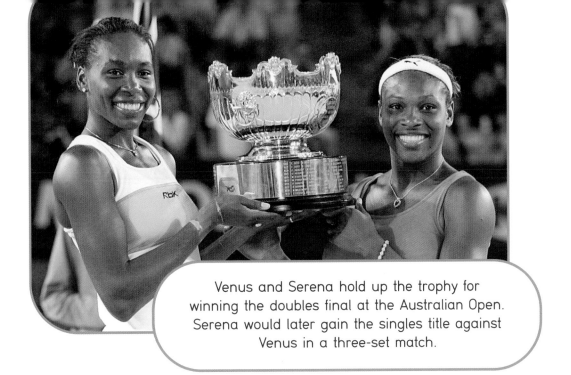

Venus and Serena hold up the trophy for winning the doubles final at the Australian Open. Serena would later gain the singles title against Venus in a three-set match.

In the 2003 Australian Open, Venus again faced Serena in the final. Serena won in a tough battle. After this win, Serena was the champion of all four Grand Slam events!

The sisters are having great success on the court. They are also showing fans their fashion talents by designing their own tennis outfits. Fans throughout the world are looking forward to great tennis and great style from Venus and Serena for many years to come.

Selected Career Highlights

Venus's Career Highlights

2003 Reached singles final of the Australian Open for the first time

2002 Reached number 1 ranking for the first time
Ended the year ranked number 2 (after Serena)

2001 Won singles titles at two Grand Slam events (Wimbledon and the U.S. Open, when she beat Serena) and four other tour events
Ended the year ranked number 3 on the WTA Tour

2000 Won singles titles at two Grand Slam events (Wimbledon and the U.S. Open) and at three other tour events
Won the singles gold medal at the Olympic Games in Sydney, Australia
Ended year ranked number 3 on the WTA Tour

1999 Won singles titles at six tour events
Ended the year ranked number 3 on the WTA Tour

1998 Won singles titles at three tour events
Beat Serena in their first professional matchup in the opening round of the Australian Open
Ended the year ranked number 5 on the WTA Tour

1997 First woman since 1978 to reach the finals at her first U.S. Open appearance
Ended the year ranked number 22 on the WTA Tour

Serena's Career Highlights

2003 Won singles title at the Australian Open for the first time
Along with Grand Slam wins from 2002, held titles in all four events

2002 Won singles titles at three Grand Slam events (the French Open, Wimbledon, and the U.S. Open), all against Venus
Reached number 1 ranking for the first time (replacing Venus). Ended year ranked number 1
Named Female Athlete of the Year by the *Associated Press*

2001 Won singles titles at two tour events
Ended the year ranked number 6 on the WTA Tour

2000 Won singles titles at three tour events
Ended the year ranked number 6 on the WTA Tour

1999 Won singles titles at one Grand Slam event (U.S. Open) and four other tour events
Ended the year ranked number 4 on the WTA Tour

1998 Ended the year ranked number 20 on the WTA Tour

1997 Entered the WTA Tour ranked number 453; three weeks later, she was ranked 102. Ended the year ranked 99

Venus and Serena's Doubles Play Highlights

2003 Won women's doubles title at the Australian Open for the second time

2002 Won women's doubles title at Wimbledon for the second time

2001 Won women's doubles title at the Australian Open

2000 Won women's doubles gold medal at the Olympic Games in Sydney, Australia
Won women's doubles title at Wimbledon

1999 Won women's doubles title at two Grand Slam events (the French Open and the U.S. Open) and one other tour event

1998 Venus won mixed doubles titles (when she paired with Justin Gimelstob) at two Grand Slam events (the Australian Open and the French Open).
Serena won mixed doubles titles (when she paired with Max Mirnyi) at two Grand Slam events (Wimbledon and the U.S. Open).
The sisters won women's doubles titles at two other tour events.

Glossary

Center Court: at a tennis stadium, the main court, surrounded by the best seats, where the most important matches are played

doubles: a tennis match in which two-person teams play each other

endorse: to help sell products by appearing in ads on television or in magazines. The company that makes the products pays money to the person endorsing the products.

final: the last match in a series of tennis matches. The winner of the final match claims the championship for that year.

ghetto: an area of a city in which a specific group of people live

Grand Slam: in tennis, the name given to four championships played around the world each year. The events are the Australian Open, the French Open, Wimbledon (in England), and the U.S. Open.

match: a tennis contest that is won when one player or team wins a specified number of games and sets

prime time: the evening hours when the largest group of people will be watching television

professional: being able to play in tournaments for money

serve: a hit of the tennis ball to start a tennis game

set: in a tennis match, a group of six or more games. A set must be won by at least two games or in a tiebreaker. Women's tennis matches have a maximum of three sets. The person who wins two of the sets wins the whole match. Winning two sets in a row is called winning in straight sets.

singles: a tennis match that pits one player against another

tennis tour: the yearly schedule, or circuit, of tennis tournaments held around the world. Professional players don't have to play in all the tournaments, but they must play in enough to keep up their tennis ranking.

tournament: a series of contests in which a number of people or teams take part, hoping to win the championship final

U.S. Open: The American Grand Slam event played every September in New York. Players from around the world compete to win the U.S. Open final in singles and doubles.

Women's Tennis Association (WTA): the governing body of professional women's tennis players. The WTA determines tennis rankings. The rankings show how well a player is playing compared to other players.

Further Reading & Websites

Aronson, Virginia. *Serena & Venus Williams*. New York: Chelsea House, 2001.

Bankston, John. *Venus Williams: Tennis Champion*. Bear, DE: Mitchell Lane Publishers, Inc., 2003.

Feldman, Heather. *Venus Williams*. New York: Powerkids Press, 2002.

Flynn, Gabriel. *Venus and Serena Williams*. Chanhassen, MN: The Child's World, 2001.

Miller, Marc. *Beginning Tennis*. Minneapolis, MN: Lerner Publications Company, 1995.

Stewart, Mark. *Venus & Serena Williams: Sisters in Arms*. Brookfield, CT: The Millbrook Press, 2001.

WTA Tour
<http://www.wtatour.com>
The official website of the WTA tour, with rankings, late-breaking news stories, biographies, photographs, and more

Sports Illustrated for Kids
<http://www.sikids.com>
The *Sports Illustrated for Kids* website that covers all sports, including tennis

Venus and Serena Fan Website
<http://www.venusandserena.homestead.com>
This website provides fans with recent news stories, biographies, photographs, and more.

Index

Photo Acknowledgments

Photographs are used with the permission of: © Jamie Squire/Getty Images, pp. 4, 5, 6, 7; © Ken Levine/Getty Images, pp. 8, 11, 12, 14, 15; © Joseph Sohm/ChromoSohm, Inc./CORBIS, p. 10; © Al Bello/Getty Images, pp. 17, 19; © Reuters/NewMedia Inc./CORBIS, p. 18; © Gary M. Prior/Getty Images, pp. 21, 25, 28 (top); © Clive Brunskill/Getty Images, p. 22; © SportsChrome East/West, Rob Tringali Jr., p. 24; © Pascal Le Segretain/Getty Images, p. 26; © Sean Garnsworthy/Getty Images, p. 27; © Duomo/CORBIS, p. 28 (bottom).

Cover: © Gary M. Prior/Getty Images (both).